Some Ether

Books by Nick Flynn

Some Ether

A Note Slipped under the Door (coauthored with Shirley McPhillips)

Blind Huber

Another Bullshit Night in Suck City

Alice Invents a Little Game and Alice Always Wins

The Ticking Is the Bomb

The Captain Asks for a Show of Hands

The Reenactments

My Feelings

Some Ether

Nick Flynn

Graywolf Press

Publication of this volume is made possible in part by a grant provided by the Minnesota State Arts Board through an appropriation by the Minnesota State Legislature, and by a grant from the National Endowment for the Arts. Significant support has also been provided by the Bush Foundation; Dayton's, Mervyn's, and Target stores through the Dayton Hudson Foundation; the McKnight Foundation; and other generous contributions from foundations, corporations, and individuals. To these organizations and individuals we offer our heartfelt thanks.

Additional funding for this title was provided by the Jerome Foundation.

Special funding for this title was provided by a grant from the Greenwall Fund of The Academy of American Poets.

Published by Graywolf Press
250 Third Avenue North, Suite 600
Minneapolis, Minnesota 55401
All rights reserved.

www.graywolfpress.org

Published in the United States of America

ISBN 978-1-55597-303-2

10   12   14   16   17   15   13   11   9

Library of Congress Catalog Card Number: 99-067244

Cover design by Scott Sorenson
Cover photograph by Marian Roth

Acknowledgments

Grateful acknowledgment is made to the editors of the following journals and anthologies where certain of these poems, sometimes in earlier versions, first appeared:

ARK/angel Review: "Sudden," "Some Ether," "And Then, And Then," "Curse"
The Marlboro Review: "God Forgotten"
Mudfish: "Angelization"
The Nation: "Bag of Mice," "Cartoon Physics, part 1"
New England Review: "Flashback"
Painted Bride Quarterly: "Ago," "Trickology," "Residue"
The Paris Review: "Fragment (found inside my mother)"
Passages North: "Flood," "Worthless"
Pierogi Press: "Salt," "My Mother Contemplating Her Gun"
Ploughshares: "You Ask How," "Emptying Town"
Provincetown Arts: "Father Outside"
Shankpainter: "The Captain Asks for a Show of Hands," "Prayer," "Elsewhere, Mon Amour," "The cellar a machine whirring through the night," "Splenectomy," "Twenty-Pound Stone," "The Robot Moves!"
The Sow's Ear Poetry Review: "1967"
Talula: "No Map"
Third Coast: "Wild with Dandelions & Roses," "Seven Fragments (found inside my father)"

"Sudden" also appeared in *What Have You Lost?*, edited by Naomi Shihab Nye, published by Greenwillow Books, 1999.
"Peach" appeared in *Cape Discovery: The Provincetown Fine Arts Work Center Anthology,* edited by Bruce Smith and Catherine Gammon, published by Sheep Meadow Press, 1994.

"Bag of Mice," "Emptying Town," "Cartoon Physics, part 1," and "Cartoon Physics, part 2" also appeared in *The New American Poets: A Bread Loaf Anthology*, edited by Michael Collier, published by the University Press of New England, 2000.

"Fragment (found inside my mother)," "God Forgotten," "Bag of Mice," and "Emptying Town" also appeared in *American Poetry: The Next Generation*, edited by Gerald Costanzo and Jim Daniels, published by Carnegie Mellon University Press, 2000.

Many friends and teachers have read all or parts of this book in manuscript form and contributed vital encouragements, inspiration, and comments. *It wouldn't exist without you—thanks go out daily.*

Specific thanks to Rodney Phillips, Caroline Crumpacker, Paul Lentz, Rebecca Wolff, Robert Danburg, Julie Carr, Franc Graham, John Mattson, Ray Nolin, and Jacqueline Woodson—*for being here, always.* And to Fred Marchant—*for deep understanding.*

For material support and time: the Fine Arts Work Center in Provincetown, the Millay Colony, the MacDowell Colony, the Djerassi Resident Artists Program, the PEN American Center, and, of course, everyone at Graywolf.

The memory of Jody Draper, Alice Draper, Richard Booton, and Ivan Wendell Hubbard infuses this book.

Finally, to Frances Richard—*love that keeps opening.*

Contents

for Tad Flynn

I

The Visible Woman

It is joy to be hidden
but disaster not to be found.

—D.W. Winnicott

Bag of Mice

I dreamt your suicide note
was scrawled in pencil on a brown paperbag,
& in the bag were six baby mice. The bag
opened into darkness,
smoldering
from the top down. The mice,
huddled at the bottom, scurried the bag
across a shorn field. I stood over it
& as the burning reached each carbon letter
of what you'd written
your voice released into the night
like a song, & the mice
grew wilder.

Fragment (found inside my mother)

I kept it hidden, it was easy
to hide, behind my lingerie, a shoebox

above my boys' reach, swaddled alongside
my painkillers

in their childproof orange cups. I knew my kids,
curious, monkeys,

but did they know me? It was easy

to hide, it waited, the hard O of its mouth
made of waiting, each bullet
& its soft hood of lead. Braced

solid against my thigh, I'd feed it
with my free hand, my robe open

as if nursing, practicing
my hour of lead, my letting go. *The youngest*

surprised me with a game,
held out his loose fists, begging
guess which hand, *but both*

were empty. Who taught him that?

The Captain Asks for a Show of Hands

Everyday, something—this time
a French ship with all her passengers & crew
slides into the North Sea, the water so cold
it finishes them. Nothing saved
but a life ring stenciled GRACE,
cut loose from its body. A spokesman can only
state his surprise
that it doesn't happen more often.

Last August, as I rode the ferry
from here to the city, a freak storm
surprised everyone,
& the Captain, forced below,
asked for a show of hands
as to whether we should go on. A woman beside me
hid her entire head in her jacket
to light a cigarette.

For years I had a happy childhood,
if anyone asked I'd say, *it was happy*.

You Ask How

       & I say, *suicide,* & you ask
how & I say, *an overdose, and then*
she shot herself,
& your eyes fill with what?
wonder? so I add, *in the chest,*
so you won't think
her face is gone, & it matters somehow
that you know this. . .

                 & near the end I
eat all her percodans, to know
how far they can take me, *because*
they are there. So she
won't. Cut straws
stashed in her glove compartment,
& I split them open
to taste the alkaloid residue. Bitter.
Lingering. A bottle of red wine
moves each night along
as she writes, *I feel too much,*
again & again. Our phone now

       unlisted, our mail
kept in a box at the post office
& my mother tells me to always leave
a light on so it seems
someone's home. She finds a cop
for her next boyfriend, his hair
greasy, pushed back with his fingers.
He lets me play with his service revolver
while they kiss on the couch.
As cars fill the windows, I aim,

making the noise with my mouth,
in case it's them,

& when his back is hunched over her I aim
between his shoulder blades,

in case it's him.

1967

I distrust the men who come at night, sitting in their cars, their
     engines running.

The living room a dark theater behind me, I watch from the curtained
     window.

My mother is twenty-seven.

She opens the car door & bends into the overhead light but before his lips
     can graze her cheek the door closes

& the light goes out.

They sit inside & fill it with smoke.

It looks creamy in the winter night, like amber, or a newfound galaxy.

I know cigarettes can kill & wonder why she wants to die.

A picture book teaches me how to vanish. All the children are monkeys.

They plunge into the icy sea each morning to become strong.

My mother buys a Harley & I cling to her past blurry lawns.

We walk out of *Bonnie & Clyde* after Gene Hackman staggers up dead.

We listen for fire bells & drive to the scene of burning houses, to stand
     close to tragedy.

The Greeks teach me to shout into the waves so people will listen.

Trickology

She'd screw a store-bought toy head,
a *water-wiggle*, onto the end of the green hose,

that made it & me go softly berserk
twisting across the summer lawn

as if air itself were valium.

she could whisper the word burn

& I'd turn to ash

A blackberry patch grew wild off the road
to the electric transformers.

I'd fill my hat & carry them home
for her to make a lattice pie. Now she tells me

that she doesn't know how to bake, that
no blackberries ever grew around us,

that I never ate pie anyway.

not ash, really,

but the bright flecks rising from a burning
house, the family outside,

barefoot

The Visible Woman

In the dark museum we see the pump of her heart, brightening with each
           beat, her pulse big through the speakers. We listen
           until the seats fill, until the floodlights come on
           & she speaks, *Welcome, this is my body*, spinning
           slowly, her palms upturned

My brother builds a wall of airplane glue around his bed, the fumes become
           dreams as they harden, our mother reaches a cool
           washcloth to his fever, the sheet sticks to his body,
           like the canvas that forms a balsa plane

Welcome, she says, *this is my body,* says *circulation* & her veins
           light up like sick rivers, says *skin is a door*, her hair
           molded plastic, her lungs filling blue, her eggs lined up
           & waiting, even her bones glow, the marrow white fire,
           like a flashlight held in my mouth

When she died we knelt at the coffin, my brother reached a hand out to her
           cheek, *she's not even real*

And Then, And Then

As a kid I ruled, God Almighty, but it got

so tired. I delivered newspapers, had a route.

If it snowed my mother would drive, I'd read her the headlines
                as we idled between houses.

I read about a man who ate an entire car, bolt-by-bolt,
                & another who ate acid

& freaked, landing in jail

where he gouged his own eyes out. I thought
                he looked like Jesus, but a lot of people

looked like Jesus then.

Patty Hearst was robbing that bank, & Nixon
                was led away by the Army. Sometimes

before I'd make it back to the car she would start to drive
                slowly away, and I'd have to jump in on the run, as if I were
                a cowboy, or a gangster. I told her about Superman,

how he'd plough through the crust of the earth for a handful of coal
                & compress it to a diamond between his palms,
                his blue muscles straining.

I was saving money to buy her a new car.

Now it's a story I tell backwards.

Across from me on the train a man is having a dialogue with himself,
saying, *I got money, you think I don't got money, shit,*
I'm waking up tomorrow morning, going to work, I got
money, I can leave anytime, I got a hundred places to go

My Mother Contemplating Her Gun

One boyfriend said to keep the bullets

locked in a different room.
                              Another urged
        clean it
or it could explode. Larry

thought I should keep it loaded
under my bed,
                    you never know.

        I bought it
when I didn't feel safe. The barrel
                is oily,

        reflective, the steel

pure, pulled from a hole
                    in West Virginia. It

could have been cast into anything, nails
along the carpenter's lip, the ladder

to balance the train. Look at this, one
                    bullet,

            how almost nothing it is—

        saltpeter   sulphur   lead   *Hell*

burns sulphur, a smell like this.

safety & hammer, barrel & grip

I don't know what I believe.

I remember the woods behind my father's house
        horses beside the quarry

stolen cars lost in the deepest wells,
the water below
        an ink waiting to fill me.

                Outside a towel hangs from a cold line
        a sheet of iron in the sky

        roses painted on it, blue roses.

Tomorrow it will still be there.

Ago

I don't even know
     how a telephone works, how your voice reached
all the way from Iron River, fed

across wires or satellites, transformed

& returned. I don't understand
     the patience this takes, or anything
about the light-years between stars.

           An hour ago
you cupped your hands in the tub & raised them up,
     an offering of steam. Now

we're driving 66 mph
& one maple is coming up fast, on fire. I begin,
     it's like those fireworks over

the East River, but it's not enough

to say this. By the time I find the words
     it will already be past, rushing away as if falling

into a grave, drained
of electricity, the world between *something is happening*

& *something happened*. Think of an astronaut, big silver hands
& gravity boots, the effort spent

     to keep from flying off into space. Think of

the first time your grandparents listened
to a phonograph, the needle falling to black

vinyl, a song without a body. Think of the names

       you see on a map, think of these towns & rivers
before they were named, when "Liberty" & "New Hope"

were a large rock, a stand of birches. It's what

       I'm afraid of, the speed with which everything
is replaced, these trees, your smile, my mother
                    turning her back to me before work,
asking over her shoulder,
how does this look?

Radio Thin Air

              Keep the radio on softly
so it sounds like two people in the next
room, maybe
your parents, speaking calmly about something
important—a lack
of cash, the broken
cellar pump. Marconi believed
we are wrapped in voices, that waves
never die, merely space themselves
farther & farther apart,
passing through the ether he imagined
floating the planets. But wander
into the kitchen & no one
will be there, the tiny red eye of the radio, songs
that crawl through walls,
voices pulled from air. Marconi
wanted to locate the last song
the band on the deck of the *Titanic* played,
what Jesus said
on the cross, he kept dialing
the frequency, staring across the Atlantic,
his ear to the water,
there, can you hear it?

Sudden

If it had been a heart attack, the newspaper
might have used the word *massive*,
        as if a mountain range had opened
            inside her, but instead

it used the word *suddenly*, a light coming on

in an empty room. The telephone

fell from my shoulder, a black parrot repeating
        something happened, something awful

    a sunday, dusky. If it had been

terminal, we could have cradled her
as she grew smaller, wiped her mouth,

    said good-bye. But it was *sudden*,

how overnight we could be orphaned
& the world become a bell we'd crawl inside
& the ringing all we'd eat.

Emptying Town

—after Provincetown

Each fall this town empties, leaving me
drained, standing on the dock, waving *bye-*
bye, the white handkerchief
stuck in my throat. You know the way Jesus

rips open his shirt
to show us his heart, all flaming & thorny,
the way he points to it. I'm afraid
the way I miss you

will be this obvious. I have

a friend who everyone warns me
is dangerous, he hides
bloody images of Jesus around my house

for me to find when I come home—Jesus
behind the cupboard door, Jesus tucked

into the mirror. He wants to save me
but we disagree from what. My version of hell
is someone ripping open his
shirt & saying,

look what I did for you.

II

Oceanic

The ocean is always looking
for a way into your boat.

—The U.S. Coast Guard, on lifesaving

Angelization

When a plane goes down we search the wreckage
for the black box, where the pilot's voice
lies: any hint
he saw the mountain rise up, if the gauges
functioned. The word for the process
by which any technology disembodies us
is *angelization:* a telephone can do it, computers
dense with blue chatter,
a television burning with the dead
who refuse to stay dead. The day Richard left
a woman sat in the waiting room, balancing
a goldfish on her knee
in a knotted plastic bag. The woman
seemed hypnotized by reruns, the goldfish
circled, always surprised by
the bag, as if expecting the water
to simply go on & on. Richard
was trying to speak—outside
a river flowed, lined with trees
beginning to bud, reflecting
in each of his eyes. I said,
squeeze my hand if you understand, but his hand
was quiet. Imagine him as a pilot, orbiting
forever, refueling midair. How could we know
the plane would fall, his body
dematerialize, fade. First we see
his hand, then the bones in his hand, then
the wheel behind the bones—an answering
machine in an empty room that whispers,
I'm not here right now. . .

Cartoon Physics, part 1

Children under, say, *ten*, shouldn't know
that the universe is ever-expanding,
inexorably pushing into the vacuum, galaxies

swallowed by galaxies, whole

solar systems collapsing, all of it
acted out in silence. At ten we are still learning

the rules of cartoon animation,

that if a man draws a door on a rock
only he can pass through it.
Anyone else who tries

will crash into the rock. Ten-year-olds
should stick with burning houses, car wrecks,
ships going down—earthbound, tangible

disasters, arenas

where they can be heroes. You can run
back into a burning house, sinking ships

have lifeboats, the trucks will come
with their ladders, if you jump

you will be saved. A child

places her hand on the roof of a schoolbus,
& drives across a city of sand. She knows

the exact spot it will skid, at which point
the bridge will give, who will swim to safety
& who will be pulled under by sharks. She will learn

that if a man runs off the edge of a cliff
he will not fall

until he notices his mistake.

Memento Mori

A virus threads its way through us, rides our blood
like a subway, erasing everything. But it's

alright, I don't want to remember floorplans or
thresholds anyway, the light
finding the airspace around my mother's door,

the black air filling her lungs

until all inside her
hangs darkly. I left the attic
unlatched, shimmied up the gutterpipe, I knew

I'd never wake her, no matter how hard I
knocked.

She opened herself like a time-lapsed rose. I thought
our bodies were mostly water

but there was so much blood. I rinsed the rags

in the sink & she whirlpooled
away, below my feet, filling sewers,

so much flowing from that moment, that
Atlantic.

All the payphones hang stuffed with quarters,
the map has been folded too many times.

I'm sick of God & his teaspoons. I don't want

to remember her
reaching up for a kiss, or the television

pouring its blue bodies into her bedroom.

I'd stare at the dust lit up by the sun,
it formed fallen pillars
connecting the windows to the floor & I knew

they were all that kept the walls
from collapse.

Flood

The earth smells like whatever drifts past—
a moment ago, black apples, now

sheep, legs turned to the sky, as if the world
had been turned over & it was me
hanging underwater. I've moved upstairs. Next it'll be

the attic, then out
onto the roof. In grade school I heard
clouds could weigh three tons & I wondered

why they didn't all just fall to the ground. Lately

I study rain, each drop shaped
like a comet, ten million of them, as if a galaxy

had exploded above us. The water now
waits to re-enter heaven, waits in my

kitchen, fattening phonebooks, bleeding
family photographs. Yesterday
the river broke its banks
& flooded the cemetery, washing away

topsoil, collapsing tombstones. It lifted

the caskets from their graves,
left someone's mother in a tree, delivered a stillborn

to the wrong family. Ten strangers
floated into the parking lot & lined their caskets up

as though anxious for the ruined market
to open. I filled sandbags, bought
another pump, read a manual on lifesaving—the trick:

hang lifelessly & breathe only air.

Flashback

Erupting is simply what volcanoes do.
— Heinz Pagels

I imagine I just barely escaped, repeat,

　　barely. . . escaped

but, more & more lately, it isn't clear
from what. The house, as

　　unlikely as it seems,

still stands, though no one inside
remembers me. In my memory it is always raining,
& when it rains

the water rises in the crawlspace
& threatens the furnace

which cost eighteen hundred dollars

new. The plumber's name penciled on
the unpainted plaster, the phone

screwed to the wall, John
smashes it up in another flashback,
　　but is this his flashback now

or mine? Last summer I tracked him down

to the woods upstate. He didn't remember
the years he lived with us, not
clearly. He asked, *did you people even know*

I'd been in Vietnam? In my flashback

he shoots out all the windows, splinters
a chair, cuts his hand deep

putting it through a cabinet door.

By morning I find blood pooled on the yellow
linoleum. It is quiet. He is
gone. In my version

it's raining that morning, the rain

drops a blanket on the house, I poke a finger
through soggy wool, press my

mouth to the holes to breathe. Where

is my mother in all this? Two lights
embedded in the kitchen ceiling—one

or the other always burned-

out. She stands at the sink, looking out
at the rain, the dead bulb

pushing down on her shoulder. Even if I could ask
she might not remember it this way. *I don't*

     think about him at all anymore, my brother

claims, while John busts up the house
for the umpteenth time, & behind locked doors

we hunker down, yelling, *Leave.*

No Map

Ghost stars convincingly stutter,
you can stare all night

& they might not even exist. As we line up
the teacher asks, *Is there a sign that says*
touch the wall? Then don't

touch the wall. On the radio a man sings, *I'm*
gonna make you love me,
but he doesn't say how. We scour

pornography, study bodies like maps

of lost & distant countries. We all have
nightmares—a man's voice

getting closer, a woman hovering
just out of reach. Mary

smears lipstick on my ears
as I search for her clitoris, having read

that if I apply the perfect balance

of thumb & forefinger
she will love me forever. In school

they give a test: *Please _____ me*

a napkin, _____ the wagons up the hill. We learn
that all the salmon are becoming

confused, that the center of the earth is a planet
spinning within a planet, & the universe
is smaller than expected,

yet filled with more
than we ever imagined. *Please*

sing me a napkin, plant the wagons
up the hill.

Wild with Dandelions & Roses

Like sands through the hourglass, the tv
intones, every weekday at 3,
bending my grandmother into her stories, trapping me

on the swirling rag carpet
as I drive my matchbox camaro

to the stitched center & back. Saturdays
Tarzan fills the room & I learn

about quicksand, how the less you struggle

the slower you sink.

⌒

Here is her hallway, the lightswitch buried

under years of wallpaper, so many layers
the corners are rounded, the walls springy,
like the earth beneath an ancient cedar. Her yard is wild

with dandelions & roses, her fingers gnarled

from turning over flowerbeds, from crushing
Japanese beetles. She gives me clorox
        to pour on anthills

& popsicles in the summer, her sidedoor
unlocked for me at night. She gives

her couch when it rains & the sound of her
breathing. Leaning over the sink,

moths powder themselves fluorescent,
she says I can have anything

once she is dead.

⌇

She tells a story of how I swallowed a wasp,
                    I don't remember

but I always felt a nest building
inside me, like I was made

of paper & spit. I make small cuts in my
                    forearm, as if to let

something out, as if to look
inside. I patch myself with flesh-colored band-aids
& she never asks why.

⌇

Down here the walls a foot thick with slits
cut through for windows.
She stands at the top cellar step,
          whistling. I smell raked grass, hear

an engine, a blade. Her teeth

float, lit by the radio dial, her shoes
line the floor of her closet,

a bodiless army ready to march.

Other Meaning

Coming home from the drive-in, asleep under
blankets in the vast backseat,

my mother full of attention to the road
& we're all wrapped in darkness & steel. Somewhere

lost in the heart of the engine

small fires burn, pushing us away
from where we've been—

the 100-foot-high movie screen
& the airplane that passed through

Steve McQueen's head. My feet stab

at my brother's, wandering his own walled city
of sleep, suspended in an endless present,

endless protection & the low hum of static.
I remember a chair, a maroon &

velvet throne,
I fell asleep in it once

under a glacier of coats
as a party raged around me. Only later did I learn

the other meaning of *maroon*—

of sailors, whole families, put out to sea
in inadequate lifeboats, left to drink their own piss

& pull gulls from the sky. I open one eye
but cannot identify the tops of passing trees.

How far to home? Once

she left me on the side of the road & drove off
into the rare green earth, her taillights

fading sparks. Once she cast me out
onto the porch, naked in the snow, merely because

I said she wouldn't dare.

The Robot Moves!

I pretend I'm afraid, carrying you
on my hip beneath the Cathedral of St. John
the Divine, past all the dead saints, the floor
dug up to lay pipe. I stop suddenly,
gasping at a darkened corner & whisper,
what was that? & your tiny hand
touches my face to soothe me
& you say, *it's alright,*
there's nothing there. As a kid
I made up a game
where I would turn into a robot,
cruel & lifeless, & it wouldn't matter
if you were my best friend, I'd turn on you
as fast as switching off a light, I'd
come after you, no matter how much you'd plead,
I don't want to play this game, because
something inside had turned, something
essential, that couldn't be repaired
with words, like those days I'd come home at dusk
my mother alone at the kitchen table,
she'd look at me over her wine
& say only, *So?*
like *I* was the stranger.

How Do You Know You're Missing Anything?

When I see a car the same model as the last car
my mother owned, a Dart the green

of a '70s refrigerator, I remember how,
after she'd gone off to bed, I'd

secretly borrow it
& drive, underage, to the harbor

& beyond, past the mansions along Jerusalem
Way, then up around the cliffs, past the doomed

summer houses, with the sea, every year, eroding
closer. I knew to just keep

going, that there were roads connecting all the way
to Mexico, & that some people did, they just
left, it happened

all the time, never seen

or heard from again. You could wander the entire
eastern seaboard, my father did,

in his woodgrain Ford, the car he one day
walked away from after
it caught fire, walked away while it was still

burning. He left us
or was thrown out, still unclear

which, & we ended up
in that yellow house, with encyclopedias

& Shakespeare
unopened for years,
as the ice in the freezer

thickened, pushing the door open

until the space inside was not big enough
for even a fist.

III

Devil Theory

Ruin is Formal—Devil's work
Consecutive and slow—

—Emily Dickinson

Seven Fragments (found inside my father)

Fragment #1

> birds sing above my bench while the city
sleeps   their chatter
wakes me

Fragment #2

> one doctor asks if I hear things
other people don't
> > one said *frostbite* said
all your toes said *amputate*

but I walked

Fragment #3

before my eyes shut I see the dog-star
crawl across absolute zero

Fragment #4

words come to me in my sleep but they don't
> sound like me   I write
we are put on this earth to help other people . . .

> why don't you answer?

Fragment #5

                  shelters,
      shitsville

Fragment #6

       gentlemen, it's that time again

      & we rise as one
line the stairwell in our white
               johnnies, a number

tied to our wrists

Fragment #7

      yes, I hear things

Glass Slipper

December 4th—
My father calls so I can wish him
a happy birthday. The next day
        he calls again
for the same reason. He sends a photograph of himself
as a salvation army santa, cold beside a black pot,
            ringing a bell.

        The first time I saw him
sleeping on a bench, sunbleach & chill,
I watched him rise, stagger to the edge of the river
            & piss, his cock
wild in his hands. Today

        outside *The Glass Slipper*
he pokes through a trashbarrel: inside
the music ends & a woman stops her dance
            to pass through a beaded curtain
& pick out the next song. Each bent note

hangs over the empty stage
dissolving into the smoke & lamé until
            she returns, picking it up
slowly from where she left off,

as if she had her whole life to unhook
        her bra, to subdue

the spotlight, to step out of
her sequined panties.

Father Outside

A black river flows down the center
of each page

& on either side the banks
are wrapped in snow. My father is ink falling

in tiny blossoms, a bottle
wrapped in a paperbag. I want to believe
that if I get the story right

we will rise, newly formed,

that I will stand over him again
as he sleeps outside under the church halogen
only this time I will know

what to say. It is night &
it's snowing & starlings
fill the trees above us, so many it seems

the leaves sing. I can't see them
until they rise together at some hidden signal

& hold the shape of the tree for a moment
before scattering. I wait for his breath
to lift his blanket

so I know he's alive, letting the story settle

into the shape of this city. Three girls in the park
begin to sing something holy, a song
with a lost room inside it

as their prayerbook comes unglued

& scatters. I'll bend
each finger back, until the bottle

falls, until the bone snaps, save him

by destroying his hands. With the thaw
the river will rise & he will be forced
to higher ground. No one

will have to tell him. From my roof I can see
the East River, it looks blackened with oil

but it's only the light. Even now
my father is asleep somewhere. If I followed

the river north I could still
reach him.

Salt

A woman stands before us   a man drowning in her poem

she reads   *I'm tired of writing about fishermen*

a man in front fights sleep   his arms folded his eyes

a doll's eyes   slowly closing   until his head

whiplashes the air   rousing he

focuses on one word   the word *salt*

until his chin drops again to his chest   I think

this is how my father moves through life

drifting off   then righting himself   a few lucid moments

maybe a week   standing outside a building he once lived in

searching his pockets for the key   The poet whispers

the ocean is always looking for a way into your boat

the sea lifts itself   everyone   thrown overboard

the man's head breaks the surface   just long enough for a mouthful

then back under   *the overwhelming silence beneath the waves*

It could be me   up there   my father drowning in his chair

I could stand before him all night   trying to find one

word   precise   a rock slipped into his open mouth

to weigh him under   away

Sunday

Scrape
the ashes from the windows, burn something
in a bowl. In another city

my father rises from his stone mattress,
                his vinyl bag a tourniquet
knotted to his wrist. Like oil

fingers leave on doorknobs, sweat
        on a cold bottle.
The blue heart on the stove wavers,

the water that fills the kettle comes from a mountain
                I've never seen. Steam

from the shower mingles with this steam, your kisses
dissolve from my chest.

Those fingerprints on the formica, I
keep opening the refrigerator, hoping for something

overlooked, edible.

Sunday. A steady bell
calls my neighbors from their doors, my father
        roused by the faithful.

I could take you to the house I grew out of,
                my mother's name inked
off the bell. Trees push up from below

the trees I remember—a woman paces the kitchen,
        a child grows inside her. I put on
my plaid secondhand coat, it holds the shape

        of someone who may or may not be dead,
          his unreadable name
sewn into the lining. Wind fills the trees above us

with rattlesnakes, as the leaves let go, making room
for more leaves.

Two More Fragments

Fragment #8

              I was a mason,
kneeling before an unfinished
wall,
          washing brick

with acid. The lime from the mortar
          steeled my fingertips

numb—even those nights I

made it home

          & held your breasts to my mouth
I was afraid, unsure
where my fingers ended

          & you began.

Fragment #9

My Alcatraz. My *Titanic*.

I sit in my cage, work the button.
Button Man.

let the prisoners in   let the guards out

          Tidal, nearly.

If a prisoner escapes
I will have to serve that man's time.

Lexington Federal. A great ship
in the middle of the prairie.

All around the sea rages.

Curse

Let the willows drop their branches, heavy with ice,
      let the sound be a whipcrack across the fields.

Let each tree be felled, let them dynamite the stumps.

From now on you will have to keep moving, from now on
      you will carry everything you own.

You will sleep beneath a payphone, dream of a room, a field.

Let the field burn clean, let your children beat the flames
      with brooms.

You will feign sleep as the conductor passes.

The names of your children will break up in your mind.

Let the stones jam the plough, let the barn fall.

Let the paint leech into the well.

Man dancing with a paper cup

Don't you know there ain't no devil
there's just God when he's drunk.
                                    —Tom Waits

You still send letters but I know

you are dead, I see you
wandering the streets when I go back home,

& I swear I am never going back. A glance
in the trash, a barrel on fire, my hands

pass right through you. You wrote
from prison but I couldn't remember
how you looked

so the bars became *cheekbone, shadow,*
lash, pressed
tightly to your face. Maybe

the silence you move through
shaped me, the way

a church bell ringing resonates

long after the ear ceases to perceive it,

the way waves space themselves
until they stop.

Prayer

Who are you talking to? she asks, the room empty.

Stylite (fragment #10)

Go into the desert sometime
climb a pole & sit up there
            for thirty-eight years or so

until the faithful start to call you a saint.

Spend your days waiting for pilgrims
bearing olives & bread, a jar of water
balanced on a woman's head
            the dipper like the tongue of a forgotten bell.

Go to the desert for half your life
then see if God doesn't find the time.

Elsewhere, Mon Amour

Leaning from the platform, waiting for a glimmer
to braid the rails

the eyes of the action hero cut from the poster

all that concrete pressing down

A fine edge gleams around your body
as if it could be contained

The way each finger is licked, dipped in &
rubbed across the gums

until the teeth go away
Even my hands kiss you

A night broken down into grains

If you find yourself lost, dig

a cave in the snow, quickly
you need shelter against the night

A candle could keep you alive
the engine of your lungs

will heat the air around you, someone will
miss you, they will send out dogs

You must be somewhere, right?

IV

Ether

It is a very beautiful world.
I never noticed before.

—John Brown, on his way to the scaffold

Cartoon Physics, part 2

Years ago, alone in her room, my mother cut
    a hole in the air

& vanished into it. The report hung &
    deafened, followed closely by an over-

whelming silence, a ringing
    in the ears. Today I take a piece of chalk

& sketch a door in a wall. By the rules
    of cartoon physics only I

can open this door. I want her
    to come with me, like in a dream of being dead,

the mansion filled with cots,
    one for everyone I've ever known. This desire

can be a cage, a dream that spills
    into waking, until I wander this city

as a rose-strewn funeral. Once
    upon a time, *let's say*, my mother stepped

inside herself & no one
    could follow. More than once

I traded on this, until it transmuted into a story,
    the transubstantiation of desire,

I'd recite it as if I'd never told anyone,
    & it felt that way,

because I'd try not to cry yet always
    would, & the listener

would always hold me. Upstairs the water
    channels off you, back

into the earth, or to the river, through pipes
    hidden deep in these walls. I told you the story

of first learning to write my own name, chalk
    scrawl across our garage door,

so that when my mother pulled it down I'd
    appear, like a movie.

The cellar a machine whirring through the night

Hovering near the ceiling, turning off
& on, & on & off, my body filling

a hundred boxes below me, I watch as we

make love. We seem good at it.
You still here? you ask,
stopping.

come into focus
I came into focus in an alley in Morocco

the moment Muhammad turned the opium knife
on me.

What was it my mother told me?
I don't care what they teach you at school

I want you to bicycle into *the flow*
of oncoming traffic
so you'll see the eyes of the man

about to run you down. The phone rings

infused with grace, my own voice
floods the darkness.

let's finish this
I come into focus lacing my boot, stumbling
over how to tie a knot.

Your ears taste like poison.
I push the knife away.

Her Smoke (her trick)

A good waitress, I wait up for her
to come home, smoky

& exhausted, her feet
swollen, I wait in her bed. Purple shadows

cross the purple carpet, her television
makes Sherlock Holmes blue, he sees
evidence everywhere

of the man who last used this room, scrapes
mud from the floor into an envelope, rich

with lime, with ash fallen
from the factories in the east. I wait.
Doze. The tv turns to snow. Silently

she pulls off her black shoes, empties
her pockets. Next, her

genie trick, blowing smoke
into an empty juice glass,

cupping it with her palm until it slowly releases
up to the ceiling, the orange

tip of her cigarette a dying

ember. We
scatter her in the Atlantic, my brother & I, I
watch her sink, diffuse. I break off

another chunk of hash, impale it
on a common pin pushed up

through the cover of *Abbey Road*, set it on fire
under an upturned glass
& we take turns taking it in, our lips
to the tilted rim. Then we fall

back in our chairs, we never
talk about her, as if even her name
were ash

& might turn to paste in our throats.

Splenectomy

Hard after the spill to again
pick the motorcycle up, to go back into
the elephant grass, the air inside
green but for the oil, hard
to get up sometimes, even after
a year, each bone un-
centered, stricken sideways, airless
beside the fallen. Go, lay
the bike back in its broken slick,
wave the cars on, something hot
sparks your face, her cry off
left, *there*, like
sex, you've forgotten her
wrist, go toward it. Tall grass, hairpin,
adrenaline, what makes it so
fast, how hands end up inside you,
how this is supposed to save you?

Five Hundred Years

                                        In
sleep our hands find each other. Outside,

the street, paved with bottlecaps—yesterday
a parked car glistened, now—a mere scatter

of green shattered glass. You murmur

from a dream, I feel
night press on my chest, like the earth
tamping the dead back into earth. If we had five

hundred years to work this out,
if after all that time

we remembered, if we still cared, if we
had fingers to dig, if there were shovels,

we could find each other, blood
compressed to rubies, lungs to slate,

fingers gone yellow, blue leaking
from your eyes, my shoes, side-

by-side beneath the window
as if I had simply
disintegrated out of them, yours,

toe-to-heel, as though you struggled.

Worthless

                    My fingers
cling to your shoulder blades now
until fucking becomes
an urging, a way to shake you, gently. How

can I tell you I don't feel
safe, when inside
a man holds bars before his face

believing himself into a prison,
when parrots fly from his open mouth
as he tries to speak, repeating *worthless,*

worthless? I'm trying to love you

but I don't know how, & then
I start to remember—we are locked together
& pushing, pushing.

Soft Radio

I don't know if Ivan is dead & I don't know

who to ask. Thin
the last time I saw him, yellow, the hospital
made him yellow. Percodan

made two of him,
one aching from the stitches, one

hovering above, whispering

it's alright, it's alright. Demerol
flattened the doctors into playing cards,
shattering

as they fell on top of him. Behind each—
outerspace, release. At 17: crystal

meth, we loved
the ring of it, like a girl's

name, like a jewel. We stole candles
& a crowbar, tore
the plywood off a ruined beachhouse

to spend the night in a tilted room. We knew

what to take—marijuana
made the world small, a pinpoint, opium

left us in the shower, counting
tiles, valium liked to drive, liked

the red lights of traffic at night, the
heater off the window, the soft

radio. It

was easy: always a two-dollar coat
on Avenue A, you could always

sell your dog. Maybe Ivan
is still sweating, propped at his table
at Foley's, nodding

though no one is talking. His loft,
a Pompeii, holes kicked in the plaster, he

pisses out the window
leaving long yellow icicles to dangle over the heads
of businessmen. On the train today

an advertisement—
a pill rising over New York like the sun,
like redemption, radiating, promising

a clear new day,

& the city again spotless,
the Statue of Liberty, perfect clouds, the water

all clear.
I don't know if Ivan is dead. The same restlessness
walks a young man

through moving subway cars, toward
or away from someone he might love,

as a woman on the platform opens & closes
an umbrella, an enormous lung,

as a man rolls quarters between his fingers,
chanting *anyone, anyone.*

Residue

. . .he somehow takes it personally, as no one
has ever taken color before, simply for making
the object. The color is totally expended in its
realization—there is no residue.
—Rilke, from *Letters on Cezanne*

Wedged between tiny desks I must be careful. If I ask
about the eyes

the braided girl will erase them

& draw another balloon-shaped head over the first,
holding her pencil like a hammer

she will color the body yellow

& the hands will be red. The shy girl
with the cleft palette

writes about being wheeled into a machine

that takes pictures of her bones. She spells *picture* like the thing
that holds milk

or the man who throws a baseball.
When she reads her draft to the class

everyone talks about when they got hurt,
I fell off my bike, my

brother got shot. . . . Christina's book begins,

my mother comes home & all she wants is her coffee
        & tv. She works

too much. Outside

a car crosses the gravel & I'm seven years old again,
        waiting up

for my mother to make it home from work. I dig a hole
        in the backyard

& sing a little song into it. Raven writes, *my grandmother*
        tucks me in at night,

draws her own head balanced on a pillow,
        while her tv whispers *yes.* Just now,

I tried to eat my orange slowly,

to sense the pulp gently untying, to savor it as if it was
        my lover's tongue, then I'm back

with this puzzle of orange skin. A boy, his desk
        isolated from the rest, asks,

is wind fast-moving air
        or something moving fast through the air?

Peach

the peach in your pocket   still damp from the faucet

its weight swings into your chest

you walk up Mechanic   the ocean still sleeping

it burns your flesh where it touches

you'll wake him up with it   press it into his eye

anytime, he said, *anytime*

a radio somewhere   the grass hasn't died

one eye shuts daylight the peach to your cheek

stippled with night   where it held to the tree

bruised where it fell hard to earth

bite away at the bruise   spit it over the fence

like whiskey his kiss like whiskey

tear away at the skin   the fruit clings to the pit

juice catches & runs in your fingers

over sandy tar lean   to take the last mouthful

wipe your chin with your hand   roll the pit with your tongue

spit it into the grass   before taking his stairs

You moved me through each room

—after hypnotherapy

All the rooms are empty, as if no one
had ever lived in them. You ask
where I am & I say, *the kitchen,*
the windows broken, the curtains
ragged, dust thick on the counters
& dead birds fill the sink. What house
& I say, *it's just a place we're staying
between houses, just a woman
my mother works with.* Find the stairs,
you tell me & I climb them on all
fours, a door off to the right,
the knob level with my eyes, I
reach up to turn it, I'd forgotten
about needing to reach. Inside my mother sits
before a mirror, fixing her hair. I lie
on the bed & watch, inside the only room
the sun seems to enter, the only room
lit up and clean. She says, *I'm going out
and I want you to be good.*
The whole time I know
I can lift my hands, open my eyes & walk
back into today, but I never try.

Fugue

If I think hard I can remember
beginning with your lips, then moving

to your eyes, then everywhere else I kissed
how sometimes after we fell asleep

we'd hold onto each other until
something inside me would waken

& my hands find your breasts
my mouth your nipples,

maybe I'd be dreaming about quicksand
& in my panic I'd reach too far overhead

for the branch that could save me & you'd half
wake up & push me away

or maybe
you'd murmur from whatever room you were

wandering, whatever bed
you were circling above, & moving to your stomach

I'd breathe you in
to my own landscape, a field overgrown

trailing on into the sky, a crow hovering around a spigot
washing its oily head, an old woman at a fork

pointing the way, until my tongue opened you &
soft birds let loose their grip on the earth

& your sleeping hands found my hair & pulled me
deeper inside & we'd imagine we were awake

& I'd forgotten who I was
but if I thought hard I could remember, beginning

with my eyes. . .

Twenty-Pound Stone

It nests in the hollow of my pelvis, I carry it with both hands, as if
　　　　　　　offering my stomach, as if it were pulling me forward.

At night the sun leaks from it, it turns cold, I sleep with it
　　　　　　　beside my head, I breathe for it.

I dream of stones.

Sometimes I dream of hammers.

I am hammering it back into sand, the sand we melt into glass,
　　　　　　　the glass we blow into bottles.

This stone is fifteen green bottles with nothing inside.

It never bleeds, it never heals, it is a soup can left on the back shelf,
　　　　　　　the label worn off.

It is the corner of a house, the beginning of a wall.

At night it changes shape, it lies on one side, casting jagged shadows.

It brightens where my tongue touches it.

Richard's eyes were this color, a pale fruit, honeydew.

When I swing it over my head I swear it could lift me.

If I jump from a bridge it would drag me down, the current couldn't
　　　　　　　carry us, it has no lungs, no pockets of air.

If I could walk it to the center of a frozen pond & leave it,
　　　　　　　in the spring it would be gone

Some Ether

I don't know if you can read this now, you
without a body, without a hand on the wheel. . . .

    For years physicists were searching outerspace
   for some ether electromagnetic waves

could travel through.

       It was Einstein who said,

  you can't find it because it isn't there. . . .

    Your hair would be gray now.

    You led me upstairs to my great-grandmother's bed
  her hair floating white above her skull
          as if it had already left her.

    I never knew her not to be blind.

She reached out to read my face
   your hands firm on my back.

    you can't find it because it isn't there

You without a body without a compass without oars
your hands are useless in this world,
       resting on my shoulders

trying to steer.

God Forgotten

God mercifully forgets us for a few hours.

A blind woman in a folding chair
rests in the sun on the sidewalk below
& for an afternoon
doesn't think about heaven. I put my hand on yours

& say, *show me,* and you begin
slowly, steadily, my hand

riding yours, a spidermonkey
holding on to its mother's back, until

your fingers disappear inside

& my fingers follow. I see myself reflected
in your face, you smile & I realize
I'm smiling also. There is so much

I want to tell you. Once I spoke to my mother
through a long cardboard tube,
put one end to her sleeping ear & the other
to my mouth & whispered,

can you hear me? She was younger
than I am now, now

she will always be younger. Another hour passes, we open
the shades. Outside
a man in a wheelchair crosses his legs. You show me

a photograph, a group of children beside a '60s
stationwagon, you ask, *can you find me?* My fingers
tangle your hair, trace
your skull, your face so radiant

I can barely look into it.

Notes

"Fragment (found inside my mother)" takes two phrases from Emily Dickinson (341).

"Radio Thin Air": The title comes from a radio program that aired on WFMU, New Jersey, in the 1990s. Marconi is the inventor of the telegraph.

"Angelization": The word was coined by Marshall McLuhan.

"The Robot Moves!" is for Esra Soroya Padgett.

"Two More Fragments": *Button Man* is the title of an unpublished novel by Jonathan Flynn.

"Residue": All worthwhile images therein are thanks to New York City public school children, to their teachers, to Lucy Calkins, and to all those at The Writing Project.

"You moved me through each room" is for Lou Krodel.

NICK FLYNN is the author of four collections of poetry, *My Feelings, The Captain Asks for a Show of Hands, Blind Huber,* and *Some Ether,* a finalist for the Los Angeles Times Book Prize and winner of the PEN/Joyce Osterweil Award for Poetry. He is also the author of three memoirs, *The Reenactments, The Ticking Is the Bomb,* and *Another Bullshit Night in Suck City,* winner of the PEN/Martha Albrand Award for the Art of the Memoir. His work has appeared in the *New Yorker,* the *New York Times Book Review,* the *Nation,* the *Paris Review,* and on National Public Radio's *This American Life.* He has won fellowships from the Library of Congress, the Provincetown Fine Arts Work Center, and the John Simon Guggenheim Memorial Foundation. He teaches in the spring at the University of Houston. He otherwise lives in or near Brooklyn.

This book was designed by Wendy Holdman. It is set in Stone Serif, a face designed by Sumner Stone and issued in digital form by Adobe in 1987 and in 1989 by ITC. Typesetting by BookMobile Design and Publishing Services. Manufactured by Versa Press on acid-free 30 percent postconsumer wastepaper.